WHAT IS DYSLEXIA?

WHAT IS DYSLEXIA?

A Book Explaining Dyslexia
for Kids and Adults to Use Together

ALAN M. HULTQUIST
Illustrations by Lydia T. Corrow

Jessica Kingsley Publishers
London and Philadelphia

First published in 2008
by Jessica Kingsley Publishers
116 Pentonville Road
London N1 9JB, UK
and
400 Market Street, Suite 400
Philadelphia, PA 19106, USA

www.jkp.com

Copyright © Alan M. Hultquist 2008
Illustrations copyright © Lydia T. Corrow 2008

Printed digitally since 2010

Library of Congress Cataloging in Publication Data
Hultquist, Alan M.
  What is dyslexia? : a book explaining dyslexia for kids and adults to use together / Alan M. Hultquist.
    p. cm.
  ISBN 978-1-84310-882-5 (pb : alk. paper) 1. Dyslexia--Popular works. 2. Dyslexic children--Popular works. I. Title.
  RJ496.A5H86 2008
  618.92'8553--dc22
                                2007038892

British Library Cataloguing in Publication Data
A CIP catalogue record for this book is available from the British Library

ISBN 978 1 84310 882 5

This book is dedicated to the children.
They show remarkable courage in facing
their reading and spelling problems every day
– and not giving up.

CONTENTS

INTRODUCTION FOR THE ADULTS

How to Use this Book

"How did I get a LD, why?"

"How can you have dyslexia, and is it contagious?"

"If I have LD does that make me a nerd?"

"My mom says that there's a smartness level. I feel like my smartness level is at – stupidity."

"Sometimes it feels like I am the only one with an LD."

"My friends sometimes say that I am stupid."

"I have Dyslexia. I am overcoming it though."

These are comments written by students with dyslexia or other learning disabilities on a website (Raskind, Margalit and Higgins 2006, see p.78)

This book is for children, but it should be used by parents, educators, counselors, psychologists, and doctors. Its purpose is to help adults explain dyslexia to children between the ages of about 8 and 11 years. It should be read with the children. It is not a book that a child with dyslexia should read alone, at least not at first. In addition, the book should not be used to try to diagnose dyslexia. That is a job for a skilled professional.

Books such as this one that help adults explain dyslexia to children and provide some answers to children's questions are important. All too often children are left "out of the loop" when it comes to discussions about the reasons for their struggles at school and what the school and their parents are going to do to help them. Frequently, no one bothers to explain to the child why she or he went through hours of tests and what the results mean. Unfortunately, this leaves it up to the child's imagination to come up with answers. Without a good explanation from adults, children tend to assume or believe that they are (to use their words) dumb, stupid, lazy, retarded, or brain damaged. Many people with dyslexia continue to believe this of themselves into adulthood.

When should you talk with a child about her or his reading problems? How old should the child be? I believe you need to let the child lead you on this. Most children begin to ask questions between the ages of 8 and 11. That is why this book was written with that age range in mind. However, every child is different. Every child will reach the point at her or his own pace where she or he will begin to ask questions about why reading is so hard or why she or he has to go to a different room during reading time. For some, it will be around the first time they are tested. For others, it may not be until they have been receiving special education services for a few years.

What should you tell the child? You do not want to overwhelm her or him, so let the child lead you on this as well. Short and simple answers may be the best ones at first. But eventually, almost all children want more detailed explanations. And that is where this book can help you. You may want to actually read the book to the child. You may want to simply read it yourself and then use the words and ideas found in it as you talk informally to the child. You will be the best judge of how and when to proceed.

It is important that parents and professionals work together. You should make sure that whomever the child speaks to first is ready. One of the questions parents need to think about is what you want to have happen if your child's first questions are directed to a teacher or school counselor. Do you want that person to answer? Do you want that person to tell your child that she or he needs to talk with you instead? Do you want the teacher or counselor to only answer your child's questions if you are also present? It is important that parents and professionals work together so the child is getting the same messages at both home and school. Therefore, you should have some plan in place, and whomever the child talks with first should let the others know.

Whether you are a parent, educator, counselor, psychologist, or doctor, before you talk with a child, you should read this entire book to yourself to make sure you understand the ideas presented. You might also want to read a book written for adults in order to help you get a deeper understanding of some issues. One such book is *An Introduction to Dyslexia for Parents and Professionals* (Hultquist 2006; see p.77). If you decide to read this book with the child, you should stop to ask questions. Make sure the child understands the words and concepts. Some of them are difficult, but I have tried to use understandable examples. You might not want to go through the whole book all at once, but instead read just one or (at the most) two chapters at a time. In addition, you might need to reread parts to the child. You should definitely use the Check It Out activities found throughout the book since many of these will help to bring the child into the process and make the book more interactive and understandable. Just be careful not to let the child see the answers first.

You will not have to read every chapter with every child. Since there are different types of dyslexia, you might only want to read the parts that have to do with the type of dyslexia the child has. On the other hand, every child will probably need to hear the information in Chapters 1, 2, 7, 8, and 9. In addition, Check It Out 9, p.48, and Check It Out 10, p.53, as well as Chapter 10, 'Answers to Questions Kids and Parents Might Ask', p.71, are also important.

The outcomes to strive for when using this book with a child should be that she or he understands the following:

1. There are many people with dyslexia.

2. It is okay to have dyslexia.

3. Dyslexia is caused by a brain difference, but her or his brain is fine and is not broken or damaged.

4. Everyone is different, everyone's brain is different, and no one does everything well. It is normal to have strengths and weaknesses.

5. She or he has strengths in addition to having trouble with reading and spelling.

6. She or he did not do anything wrong to cause the dyslexia. The child should not feel guilty. Neither should the child blame her or his parents.

7. And most importantly, she or he is smart.

When you use this book it should not be the first time the child has heard all of this. Most likely, the child went through an extensive evaluation before being diagnosed. Therefore, talking with the child about the evaluation and what it revealed is usually a good starting point before using a book such as this one. However, just as using this book should not necessarily be the first thing you do, it should also not be the last. There will be an ongoing need to discuss the child's strengths and struggles throughout her or his years at school, and perhaps even beyond that.

The Appendix at the back of this book lists various professional organizations. You can use these to find out more information. You will also find a list of some helpful books in Chapter 10, 'Answers to Questions Kids and Parents Might Ask'.

Part I

FOR KIDS

Chapter 1

MEET JAMIE

Jamie is in Grade 5. He goes to see a special reading teacher every day while his friends stay in the classroom. Other children also leave the class for different reasons, so Jamie isn't alone in needing help. But he doesn't care about that. He's not a good reader and he knows it. And it's not like reading only happens once a day when he's with Ms Sloan. He also has to read during math, science, and silent reading time. And now the PE teacher has started giving students homework to read about health and exercise! Everywhere Jamie goes, there are words he's supposed to know how to read, but can't. Reading is hard for him and it's everywhere.

Jamie used to feel good about himself. He can run and ride a bike faster than his friends, and he's an excellent football player. In fact, he's the best player on his team. He's also good at drawing, computer games, and helping his mother fix their truck. But he's no longer sure. Sometimes, he feels stupid because all his friends read better than he does. And he doesn't even want to think about spelling!

Jamie is a smart boy, but he has trouble with reading and spelling. He has this trouble because he has dyslexia (dis-LEX-ee-u). Dyslexia is a type of learning difference that makes it hard for some people to read and spell. It is often inherited (in-HER-i-tid). This means that if you have it, you might have gotten it from one of your parents, grandparents, or great-grandparents. But you didn't catch it from them the way people catch a cold or the flu. Dyslexia is not a disease and it's not something that you can get from being around someone who has it. It's usually something that you're born with. Kids inherit a lot of things from their parents and grandparents. Some examples of things children can inherit are eye color, hair color, whether their hair is straight or wavy, whether or not they can curl up the sides of their tongue, and how tall they will be when they grow up.

Check It Out 1

Talk with your parents about all the different things that you have inherited from them. You might have the same color eyes or the same color hair as they do. You might be taller or shorter than your friends, just as your parents might be taller or shorter than their friends. Your parents might both be left-handed, and you might be also. But, you might not. Kids are never exactly like their parents.

Chapter 2

WHAT CAUSES DYSLEXIA?

If you have dyslexia it means that a small part of your brain is built a little differently from other people's. But this is not bad. Everybody is different. Everybody looks different on the outside, and everybody's brain is different too. That's why everyone has

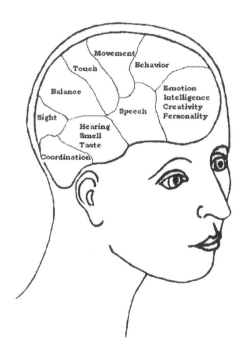

their own personal list of things they're good at and things they find hard to do. Your list is probably different from your friends' or your parents' lists. Even other people with dyslexia would not have exactly the same list as you.

Check It Out 2

Make a list of all the things you can think of that you find easy. Now make another list of the things you find hard. Have your parents, brothers, sisters, and a few friends do the same thing. You should find out that the lists are not exactly the same. That's because everyone is different. If we were all the same, life would be pretty boring, and it would cause problems. What if we were all good readers, but no one was good at fixing cars? There'd be a lot of broken cars sitting around all over the place making a mess! Or what if we were all good at fixing cars, but no one knew how to cook? We'd all be very hungry!

People don't have dyslexia because they (or their parents) did something wrong. Dyslexia is just something they have, like brown eyes or black hair. It happens because of how their brain cells work. Every part of your body is made up of cells. Cells are so small that you can't see them without using a microscope. But just because they're small doesn't mean they aren't important. They are what make your body work.

Different parts of your body are made up of different types of cells. This is important because different parts of your body have different jobs to do.

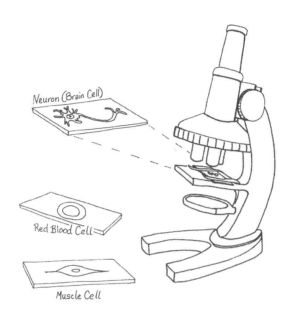

Many of the cells in your brain have a special name. They're called neurons (NUR-ons). These neurons help determine how good you are at different things. Some people's neurons work in a way that makes them really good singers, while other people's make it hard for them to sing. Some people's neurons work in a way that makes them excellent athletes, while other people's make it hard for them to be good at sports. And some people's neurons work in a way that allows them to become good readers and spellers, while other people's make it hard for them to read and spell. This isn't bad, it's just part of who they are. Everybody's brain is different and that's good.

Chapter 3

ONE KIND OF DYSLEXIA

Trouble with Sounds

There are different types of dyslexia because there are different skills that make people good readers and spellers. People can have strengths or weaknesses in any of these skills. A weakness in one skill can cause one kind of problem. A weakness in a different skill can cause a different kind of problem.

Some people with dyslexia can remember words they have seen before and that they have practiced reading, but have trouble sounding out new words. They have trouble understanding the sounds that make up words. These sounds are called phonemes (FOE-neemz). A word like **dog** has three sounds or phonemes in it. It has the /d/ sound, which we spell with a **d**; the /o/ sound, which we spell with an **o**; and the /g/ sound, which we spell with a **g**. **Dog** is a pretty easy word, but not all words are easy. For example, the word **aluminum** is a lot longer than **dog** and a lot harder to say.

Check It Out 3

Listen to these words. Then try to say them. Which ones are easy to say and which ones are hard? Which ones are short and which ones are long? Are all the long ones hard? Are all the short ones easy?

cat, house, motorcycle, jet, refrigerator, telescope, balloon, tiger, desk, run, hospital, animal, spaghetti, aluminum, bed, bathtub, rhinoceros, doghouse, car, scissors, keys, star, zipper, stethoscope, potato, baby

---

Some phonemes are harder to hear than others and it can be hard to tell the difference between some of the letter sounds. Make the sound for the letter **b**. This is the /b/ sound. (Try not to say "buh" but just /b/, like the first sound in the word **boy**.) Notice how your lips are pressed together at first, but then your mouth opens and a burst of air comes out. Now make the sound for the letter **p**. This is the /p/ sound. (Try not to say "puh" but just /p/, like the first sound in the word **pan**.) Your mouth does exactly the same thing for /p/ that it did for /b/. So how are these sounds different? Make the sounds again, but this time put your fingers over the front of your throat (in about the middle). You should feel a little vibration when you say /b/ that you don't feel when you say /p/. That vibration (which is called voicing) is the only thing that's different between these two phonemes. The vibration, or voicing, makes /b/ a little easier to hear than /p/. The sound /b/ uses your voice, but the sound /p/ is more like a quiet whisper.

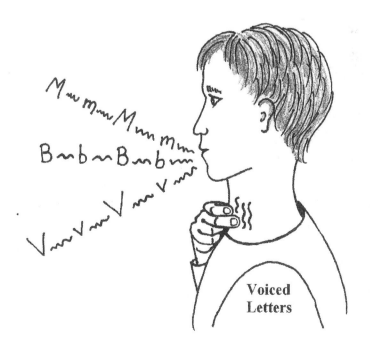

Voiced Letters

Check It Out 4

Make the sounds for these pairs of letters. Can you figure out how they're different?

k g   f v   p b   t d

s z   ch j   m n   f th

(th as in **thin**)

Answers

How did you do? The sounds for k and g are exactly the same except for voicing. You get that vibration in your throat when you make the /g/ sound, but you don't get it when you make the /k/ sound. Voicing is also the only difference between most of the other pairs of sounds (/f/ and /v/, /p/ and /b/, /t/ and /d/, /s/ and /z/, and /ch/ and /j/).

The sounds /m/ and /n/ are different because of how you place your lips and tongue. Both sounds cause a vibration in your throat, and both sounds come out your nose. (Try humming by going /mmmmmmm/ while you pinch your nose closed. You can't do it! That's because the /m/ sound comes out of your nose instead of your mouth.) When you make the /m/ sound, your lips are closed and your tongue is near the bottom of your mouth. When you make the /n/ sound, your lips are open a little and your tongue is near the top of your mouth.

The sounds /f/ and /th/ are both quiet because they do not use your voice. If you put your fingers on the front of your throat when you make them, you will not feel a vibration. These sounds are different because of how you use your tongue. Your tongue is inside your mouth for /f/, but it sticks out a little between your teeth for /th/.

Question: Can you think of another sound that the letters **th** can make? I'll give you a hint. It has to do with voicing. That's right. **Th** can sound like the beginning of **thin** or like the beginning of **the**. The only difference between these two different sounds for **th** is that vibration in your throat again.

Fact: Did you notice how sometimes I wrote just the letters and sometimes I put them inside slash marks, like this /m/? When the letter is outside the slash marks (like **m**) it means I'm talking about the letter. When the letter is inside the slash marks (like /m/) it means I'm talking about the sound the letter makes.

Make the sounds /b/ and /p/ again. Notice how they happen very fast. They are like a really fast fighter jet going by. First your mouth is just sitting there doing nothing, and then suddenly BAM! there's a really fast noise. Then the noise is gone. Just like a fighter jet flying by and disappearing, but

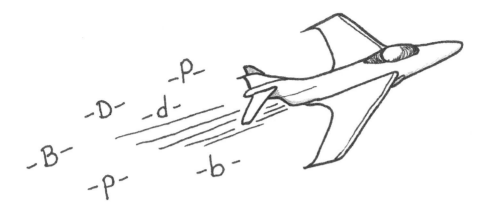

even faster! Now make the sound for the letter **m**. This is the /m/ sound. (Don't go "muh," but /mmmmm/, sort of like humming.) You can make this sound last a long time. It doesn't disappear fast like a jet, but is slower like a bicycle. It's hard to get a good look at a fighter jet when it goes by fast. But it's a lot easier to get a good look at a bicycle when someone rides by slowly.

Just as it can be hard to see a fast-moving jet very well, it can be hard for some people's brains to hear fast sounds like /b/. Now think about all the different sounds you hear every time someone talks. Listen to this sentence: **Do you want some ice cream?** How many sounds do you hear? Can you figure it out? (The answer is 17.) How many **different** sounds are in that sentence? Can you figure it out? (The answer is 14.)

Talking uses a lot of different sounds, and trying to make sense out of them can be difficult because they happen so fast. Remember the sentence **Do you want some ice cream?** There were 17 sounds in that sentence. Well, what if 17 fighter jets flew by in the same amount of time it takes to say **Do you want some ice cream?** Would you be able to figure out how many there were, what they all looked like, and if any were exactly the same? Probably not, but your brain has to figure out how many and what kinds of sounds it hears every time someone talks. And, as you can see by the fact that 17 sounds happen very quickly in a short sentence like **Do you want some ice cream**, this is a lot of work for your brain to do. Well, some people's brains have a hard time making sense out of the different sounds we use to talk because those sounds happen really fast, one right after the other.

Some phonemes are louder than others. And some phonemes are faster than others. But there's also another reason why making sense out of the sounds in words can be hard. When we talk, we don't say just one sound at a time. Listen to this word: **dog**. When we say that word, we don't say it one sound at a time like this: /d/-/o/-/g/. Instead, we join the sounds together into one group that we call a word. The sounds in words overlap with each other. That can make it hard for some people's brains to figure out how many sounds there are.

Think about it this way. If someone played three or four notes at the same time on a piano, guitar, or other musical instrument would you be able to tell how many different sounds there were and which ones they were? Probably not. Some people have the same trouble with the sounds in words. They have a hard time telling how many sounds there are and which ones they are because the sounds overlap and join together. This makes it hard for them to learn how to read and spell.

When you read and spell, you not only have to hear all the sounds, but you also have to know which ones they are and what letters go with them.

People whose reading and spelling problems are caused by difficulty understanding phonemes have trouble with **phonological** (foe-nu-LO-jik-l) **processing**. This is just a fancy way of saying that their brains try to make sense out of speech sounds in a different way from most people's. **Phonological** is a word that refers to using the sounds of language to listen, speak, or remember. **Processing** is a word that refers to what your brain does with those sounds to try to make sense out of them.

Check It Out 5

Part of phonological processing is the ability to play with the sounds in words. There are lots of ways to do this.

You can make up rhymes. Words that rhyme sound the same at the end, like **man, pan, fan**, and **plan**. You can create sentences made up of rhyming words. For example, **The man had a plan to use his pan as a fan**. You can even make up silly pairs of rhyming words, like **mouse** and **frouse**.

Another way you can play with sounds is to think of words that begin with the same sound, like **lilies, lot, left, Linda, lying, loose**, and **library**. You can also make up sentences with words like these: for example, **Linda left a lot of lilies lying loose in the library**.

You can have your parents say words broken up into small parts so you can guess what the words are. For example, if your father said the sounds /m/-/a/-/p/, would you know that the word was **map**?

You can count the number of sounds in words. This can be tricky. If your mother said the word **dog**, could you tell her that there are three sounds in it? What if she said the word **three**? There are five letters in this word, but how many sounds are there? (The answer is three.)

You can also try to think of words that differ by only one sound. For example, **bike** and **hike** have all the same sounds except at the beginning, **pat** and **pad** have all the same sounds except at the end, and **lake** and **like** have all the same sounds except in the middle.

You could have fun learning how to make pig latin words. Pig latin words are made by moving the sound at the beginning of the word to the end of it, and then adding a long **a** sound. So the word **dog** would become **og-day**. What are the pig latin words for **man, cat,** and **play**?

Answer
They are **an-may, at-cay,** and **lay-pay**.

People with this kind of dyslexia have trouble sounding out words when they read. So when they come to a word they don't know, they often have to ask someone what it is because they can't figure it out by themselves.

Sometimes they also have trouble saying words correctly. Words like **hospital, aluminum,** and **spaghetti** can be hard for some people to say.

The people with this kind of dyslexia can also have a lot of trouble spelling words well enough for other people to read them. One nine-year-old girl with dyslexia wrote this: **pesel be klai**. Can you figure out what it's supposed to say? It's supposed to be **please be quiet**. Can you figure out what mistakes she made trying to get the sounds right?

Of course, lots of kids have trouble with these things when they're learning new words and learning how to read and spell. Most of the time it does not mean they have dyslexia.

Chapter 4

A SECOND KIND OF DYSLEXIA

Trouble Remembering How Letters and Words Look

Some people with dyslexia can sound out a lot of words and can spell words by thinking of the sounds they hear, but they have trouble remembering what letters and words look like. They don't see letters and words backward, but they might have trouble remembering the difference between a **b** and a **d** or between **saw** and **was**. Also, although most people can remember a word after reading it only five or six times, some people with dyslexia cannot remember words until they have read them hundreds of times.

Making sense out of letters and numbers can be hard because we treat them differently than we do anything else. Think about what a dog looks like. A dog could be sitting or standing. It could be lying on its back or standing up on its

back legs. It could be standing with its head facing to the right or facing to the left. But no matter what it's doing or what it looks like, we still call it a dog. Letters and numbers don't work that way. If you make the letter **b** with the round part facing to the right, we call it a **b**. But, if you make it with the round part facing to the left, we call it a **d**. And if you make it upside down, it's a **p** or a **q**. This can be very confusing. You can draw a dog any way you want and it's still a dog. But you can't do that with numbers and letters. They have to be written the right way. Everyone has trouble with this when they first learn to read and write. But some people have lots of trouble remembering what different letters and numbers look like.

Words can look a lot alike too. The words **was** and **saw**, and the words **how** and **who** have the same letters, but they're in a

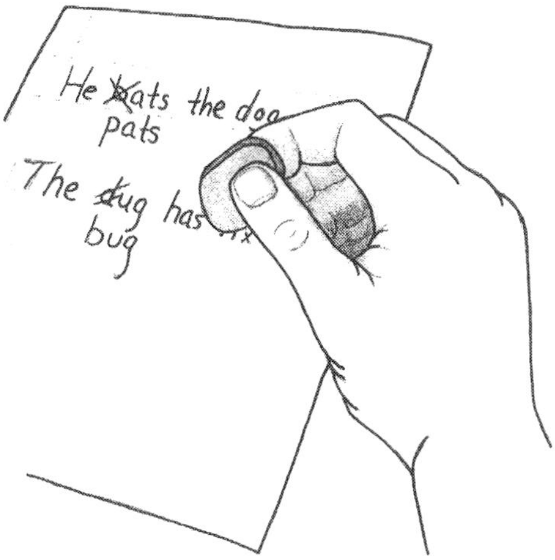

Check It Out 6

Look at these numbers and letters. Can you find the ones that are printed backwards?

И ꟻ g P Ƽ 9 Ƨ A T

Ɛ w m b ძ 2 e r ꙅ

Answers

How did you do? Did you find all the numbers and letters that were printed backwards? The backward numbers and letters are N, F, 5, S, 3, 6, and z.

different order. The words **there** and **where**, and the words **then** and **when** are the same except for the first letter. And the only difference between **though** and **thought** is that one has an extra letter at the end. When you learn to read and spell, you have to remember exactly what letters are in words and what order they come in. This can be hard.

People who have trouble remembering what words and letters look like have trouble with **orthographic** (or-thu-GRA-fik) **processing**. This is just a fancy way of saying that their brains can't remember what letters, numbers, and words look like as well as most people's. **Orthographic** is a word that refers to the letters, numbers, words, and symbols (like +, =, &) that we use when we write. **Processing** is a word that refers to what your brain does with those letters, numbers, words, and symbols to try to make sense out of them and remember them.

People with this kind of dyslexia can usually read and spell words okay as long as all the letters match the sounds. But not all words do this. To make it even more confusing, some words have letters in them that don't make the right sound. And some words have those confusing letters **b**, **d**, **p**, and **q**. One ten-year-old boy with orthographic dyslexia wrote these words: **woct, opin, bilding, qlay, tak**. Can you figure out what they're supposed to be? They're **walked, open, building, play**, and **take**. Can you see how this boy wrote down all the right sounds, but still had trouble spelling the words correctly?

Not only are there a lot of letters used to write words, but there are also a lot of different rules that go with spelling. Unfortunately, some words don't follow these rules. These words can be hard for someone with orthographic processing problems. One rule you may have learned is that when there are two vowels next to each other, the first one says its name and the second one is silent, like in the word **meat**. But not all words follow this rule. Think about the word **said**. It has two vowels next to each other, but you don't hear the letter **a** even though the rule says that you should. You don't even hear the letter **i**. When we say the word **said**, the middle of the word sounds like the middle of **fed**. It sounds like an **e**. Words that don't follow the rules can be hard because you can't sound them out. All you can do is try to remember what they look like. This is harder for some people than it is for others.

Check It Out 7

Try to read these words. Remember, one rule is that when two vowels are together, the first one says its name and the second one is silent. Which of these words follow the rule and which ones don't?

bead bread   said paid   boat broad
seen been   does goes

Answers

How did you do? The words that follow the rule are **bead**, **paid**, **boat**, **seen**, and **goes**. In all of these words, the first vowel says its name and the second vowel is silent. For some people, the word **been** also follows the rule.

When I was in school, I was taught the rule like this: **When two vowels go walking, the first one does the talking**. You need to know that this rule does not always work. In fact, it never works for words with **au**, **eu**, **oi**, **oo**, **ou**, and **oy**. But it is still a good rule to know.

Also, it can be hard for some people to remember what words to use when the words sound the same but are spelled differently. Which is something to eat, **meat** or **meet**? Which is water, **see** or **sea**? Can you remember? These words are hard because even though we say them the same way, they mean different things. You need a good memory to remember which one is which.

Some people can also have trouble when numbers look alike or when there are silent letters in words.

Of course, lots of kids make the kinds of mistakes mentioned in this chapter or have similar trouble when they're learning how to read and spell. Most of the time it does not mean they have dyslexia.

Check It Out 8

Can you tell what each of these words mean? Be careful. The words in each pair sound the same, but they mean different things.

through threw   eye I   or oar   made maid

our hour   flee flea   son sun   which witch

there their   too two   rose rows   know no

Answers

How did you do? Here are the answers.

through: to go in one end and out the other end. **Mary walked through the room**.

threw: someone tossed something. **I threw the ball to my friend**.

eye: the part of the body that lets people see things. **My sister has glasses to help her eyes see better**.

I: the word we use to talk about ourselves. **I went to the store**.

or: this word means there is a choice. **Do you want cake or pie?**

oar: A long piece of wood used to move a boat. **We used both oars to row the boat to shore**.

made: to create something. **The children made their parents a present**.

maid: a woman hired to clean a house. **The maid vacuumed the bedrooms**.

our: it belongs to us. **That is our house**.

hour: a unit of time that is 60 minutes long. **I will meet you at the mall in one hour**.

flee: to try to get away from something dangerous. **We should flee from the bear before it eats us!**

flea: a small insect that can bite and is often found on dogs and cats. **My dog scratches herself a lot because the fleas are biting her**.

son: a male child. **My parents have one son and one daughter**.

sun: the big yellow star in the sky that makes Earth warm and gives us light. **We got up early to see the sun come up over the lake**.

which: this word means there is a choice. **Which toy do you want to buy, the remote control car or the computer game?**

witch: a woman who does magic. **I dressed up like a witch for Halloween**.

there: in a certain place. **The book is over there on the table**.

their: belonging to them. **That is their car**.

too: also. **Do you want to come too?**

two: the number 2. **We have two cats and their names are Fluffy and Whiskers**.

rose: a kind of flower. It can also be a color. It can also mean to get up. **I rose out of bed so I could get dressed for school**.

rows: when things are in straight lines. **After the assembly, the principal told the students to line up in rows behind their teachers**.

know: to have information in your brain. **I know the days of the week**.

no: the opposite of yes. **No, you may not have ice cream before dinner**.

Chapter 5

A THIRD KIND OF DYSLEXIA

Trouble Finding Words

Some people with dyslexia can hear and understand all the sounds in words. They can even remember what letters and words look like. But they still have trouble reading and spelling. This is because they think of or remember letters, words, and sounds slowly.

You have lots of places in your brain where you keep information so you can find it later. Sometimes it's easy to find what you want and sometimes it's hard – just like finding toys in your room. Sometimes it's easy to find a toy when you want it (like when your room is neat), and sometimes you have to spend a long time looking for it (like when your room is a mess). Letters, words, and sounds can be the same.

You keep your memory of letters, words, and sounds stored in your brain just like you keep toys stored in your room. Have you ever looked for something in your room and not found it,

only to have someone else go in and see it right away? They might have gotten mad and told you, "It was right in front of you! How could you not see it? You just didn't try hard enough!" Well, the same kind of thing can happen with letters, words, and sounds. Let's think about words.

Sometimes you can look at a word and right away know what it is. But sometimes you see a word and you know that you've seen that word before, but it takes a while for you to remember what it is, even though you are trying your best to read it. You have to search your brain to find your memory of that word just like you sometimes have to search your room to find a misplaced toy.

Sometimes when you need to spell a word you get it right the first time. But sometimes you have to write it two or three or four times before it looks right. These kinds of things happen to everyone. But if it happens a lot, that person might have a kind of dyslexia.

People who have a lot of trouble finding words often read very slowly. They might know a word in one sentence, but have trouble remembering what it is when they see it in a different sentence. People who read slowly often have trouble remembering what they read. They spend so much time trying to read the words correctly that they can't pay attention to what the words mean.

Everyone has trouble remembering new words and everyone reads slowly sometimes. Only occasionally is the person having trouble because of dyslexia.

Check It Out 9

There are things you can do to become better if you have trouble reading quickly. You want to train your brain to recognize words right away. To do this, you have to practice reading. If you want to become a good skateboarder or a good skier, you have to practice the same skill or move over and over again. If you want to become better at playing a musical instrument, you also have to practice a lot. The same thing is true for reading. To become a faster reader you need to practice reading words, stories, and poems over and over. But, you don't want the words, stories, and poems to be too hard. You should practice with material that you can read with no more than two mistakes for every hundred words.

The words you need to practice can be put on flashcards or just typed or written on a piece of paper. You can sit down with your parents and go through a short word list four times in a row, trying to get faster each time. Your teacher can help you figure out how long the word list should be and what words to put on it. A goal to aim for is to try to read each word in no more than one or two seconds. You need to read these words aloud so your parents can hear you. You can keep track of how long it takes to read the word list and then see your growth by making a graph.

To practice reading stories and poems, you can pick a section of a book that you know really well. That section should be between 25 and 100 words long. Your teacher can help you decide how long it should be for you. You should read that same section aloud four times in a row. Again, you can keep track of your progress with a graph. After you have read the section four times, put it away and the next day you can practice with a different section of the book or with part of a new book.

You should practice reading words, stories, and poems at least four days a week, but you don't need to spend a long time on it. Five or ten minutes each day is plenty of time. Just make sure that the material is not too hard. You don't want to practice making mistakes!

Even though it is important to learn how to read quickly, you need to remember some things. First, it is never okay to read too fast. Second, sometimes it is important to read slowly, especially when you have to read books that have a lot of facts and details in them, such as this one, or science and social studies books. Third, being a good reader is more than just reading the words correctly and quickly. Good reading is also about understanding and remembering what you read. Finally, being a good oral reader also means that you pause in the right places, stress the right words, use your tone of voice to show emotions and questions, pay attention to punctuation marks, and group words together into phrases.

Chapter 6

A FOURTH KIND OF DYSLEXIA

Mixed Dyslexia

The last kind of dyslexia that we know about is called mixed dyslexia. It's called mixed dyslexia because it's a combination of some of the other kinds. This means there's more than one reason why the person is having a hard time becoming a good reader and speller. Some people have trouble with both understanding the sounds of language and with remembering what words look like. Other people have trouble with both remembering what words look like and with remembering words quickly. Some people have trouble with all three areas. There are many different combinations. Most people with dyslexia probably have some kind of mixed dyslexia.

Check It Out 10

Even if you have trouble reading, you probably enjoy listening to your teachers and parents read to you. I know I still like to hear people read aloud. You should ask your parents to read with you for at least ten minutes every day. They should read books you are interested in even if they are ones that you can't read yourself. They could read both fiction and nonfiction books to you. (Fiction books are made up. Nonfiction books are about things that are real.) Here are some ideas of things to do with your parents while they read fiction and some kinds of nonfiction books to you.

If the book has pictures (even if the only picture is on the cover), look at them before you start reading. Talk with your parents about the pictures and try to figure out what the book might be about. If there are pictures that are really interesting, talk about them. What's happening? Have you ever seen or done anything like what's happening in the picture? Is there anything in the picture that you don't know? If there is, ask your parents about it.

As your parents are reading to you, stop often to talk about what's happened. **Who** are the characters? **Where** are they? **What** are they doing? **Why** are they doing that? **How** are they doing things or how are they planning to do things? **How** do they feel? **Why** do they feel that way? Once in a while, close your eyes and try to make a picture in your head about what's happening in the stories. Making mental pictures can help you understand books better.

You should also stop occasionally to try to make predictions about what might happen. **Where** might the characters go? **How** might they try to solve a problem? **What** hints does the author give you about what's coming up?

You could also try to put yourself in the book. Talk with your parents about **what** you would do if you were one of the characters in the book. Also talk about **why** you would do that and **how** you would feel. You should also ask your parents some of these same questions to find out if they would make different decisions than you would. There are no correct answers to these kinds of questions.

If there are things in the book you don't understand or words you don't know, ask about them. If there are things in the book that are similar to things you've done, stop reading and talk about them with your parents.

If it is a long book and it takes more than one sitting to get through, start the next sitting by talking about what has happened so far. Along with your parents, try to come up with a short summary of what has happened. You could even draw pictures about things that have happened or talk about your favorite parts so far.

After you've finished the book, try to tell it back to your parents. You don't want to tell them the book word for word, but you should try to recall the important information and tell it in the order it happened. Make sure you include information about **how** characters felt, **why** they felt that way, and **why** they did certain things or made certain decisions. These kinds of information are very important parts of stories.

After you retell the story, you could write it down to practice getting your ideas on paper. You could then illustrate the summary. If there was something in the book that really interested you, you could try to find other books about it so that you can learn more.

If your parents want to know more about things they can do when they read with you, they can check out the book **How to Read with Your Children: Parent/Caregiver Guide** by Phyllis A. Wilken (see p.78).

Chapter 7

PEOPLE WITH DYSLEXIA ARE SMART AND COURAGEOUS

Sometimes, people with dyslexia have trouble with things other than reading and spelling. For example, they might have trouble with handwriting or math. They might also have trouble copying words or remembering what people say. They might have trouble with other things too. This doesn't mean they're stupid. It's just part of who they are.

Even though people with dyslexia have trouble with words, they're smart and there are things they can do well. In fact, people with dyslexia can grow up to be just about anything. For example, some adults with dyslexia are artists, actors, scientists, singers, athletes, teachers, plumbers, mechanics, doctors, and so on. Even though people with dyslexia have trouble with reading and spelling, some even grow up to be authors! There are many famous people with dyslexia (see Check It Out 11).

Check It Out 11

Famous People with Dyslexia or Signs of Dyslexia

Tom Cruise (actor)

Nelson Rockefeller
(Vice President of the US)

John Irving (author)

Magic Johnson
(basketball player)

Danny Glover (actor)

Thomas Edison (inventor)

Woodrow Wilson
(US President)

Terry Bradshaw
(American football player)

Cher (singer and actor)

Greg Louganis (Olympic
diver)

Agatha Christie (author)

Billy Bob Thornton (actor)-

Bruce Jenner (Olympic
athlete)

Whoopi Goldberg (actress)

Walt Disney (animator)

Nolan Ryan (baseball
player)

According to websites such as www.dyslexia.com and
www.dyslexia.tv these famous people had trouble with
reading and spelling.

This is so important that I want you to read it again: **People with dyslexia are smart. They just have trouble with words**. Say that out loud. Say it again. Try to remember it. You might not always feel smart, but you are.

If you have dyslexia, you might wish that you were just like your friends. You might wish that you were "normal," "average," or "just a regular kid." But you **are** all those things! Just because you have a hard time with reading and spelling doesn't mean you aren't a regular kid. If you could do everything well, you wouldn't be average, you'd be a superhero! And they're just make-believe.

You might not be a superhero, but many kids with dyslexia are heroes. There are many different kinds of heroes. A hero is

simply a person who is very brave or courageous. A lot of kids
with dyslexia show a great deal of courage every day. You need
to be courageous to spend time every day standing face to
face with your enemy. And for kids with dyslexia, it can seem as
if words are their enemy. It takes a lot of courage to spend time
every day trying to do something that's hard, and to do it
where people can see you stumble or even fail. Kids with
dyslexia have to do this at school every day. They have to read
aloud in front of their friends and they might have to let other

kids in class see their written work with all the misspelled words and messy handwriting.

It takes even more courage to spend time every day trying to do something that is hard and to not give up, but to keep trying your best. Some kids with dyslexia do give up, but many do not. Many of them keep trying their best year after year to become better readers and spellers. This requires a huge amount of courage and bravery. So, although you can't be a superhero, you can be a hero by trying to be the best reader and speller you can be, even though you might have to work at it really hard for a very long time.

.

Chapter 8

FEELINGS, HARD WORK, AND BULLIES

People with dyslexia can learn to read and spell better, but it takes a lot of hard work, and they often need to be taught differently from their friends. That's why Jamie (the boy at the beginning of this book) sees a special teacher for reading. Like

Jamie, you might be embarrassed about going to a special room for reading, but you should try not to be. Seeing a reading teacher to learn how to read is no different than seeing a music teacher to learn how to play an instrument. Both teachers are helping kids learn how to get better at something. And few people are embarrassed about seeing the music teacher.

You might be angry and think that it's not fair that you have to work so much harder than your friends do to learn how to read. And you're right. It isn't fair. Not only is it not fair, but dyslexia is a hard thing to have because words are everywhere. There's no way you can avoid them or escape them. But even though it isn't fair that you have to work so hard to learn reading and spelling, it's important for you to remember that **everyone** has to work hard to learn things, even adults. Hard work is important. It's through hard work that people get stronger. It's through hard work that people learn how to rollerblade, snowboard, paint pictures, play a musical instrument, and learn other skills. It was through hard work that you learned how to walk, swim, ride a bike, tie your shoes, and tell time. You've

always had to work hard to learn new things because that's how everybody learns. It's just that some people learn some things more easily than others.

Unfortunately, having dyslexia might mean that other kids make fun of you, tease you, or call you names. Sometimes kids get picked on because of how they look, how they dress, how they talk, how they play sports, what they like to do, or how they read. Sometimes kids get picked on for no reason at all! It is never okay for kids to pick on someone or tease them. No one is perfect and no one should be teased or made fun of for any reason. If this happens to you, it can make you feel bad and angry. You might want to say mean things back or even fight with the bully who is teasing you. But don't. Tell your parents, your teacher, your school's principal or headmaster, or your school's counselor about what is happening. Telling adults about things like bullying is never tattling. By telling an adult, you can get help. The adults can help you feel better. They can also help you learn how to respond to bullies. And they can work with the bullies to help them feel better about themselves and to learn better ways to act.

Chapter 9

THE END

If you have dyslexia, you need to know that you're not alone. There are probably one or two children with dyslexia in every classroom at your school – and in every school in the world. That's a lot of people!

If you have dyslexia, or if you know someone who is having trouble learning to read and spell, remember that they're not stupid and it's not their fault. Also remember that no one is good at everything. Everyone is good at some things but has trouble with other things. We're all different, and that's what makes the world so interesting!

Part II

FOR KIDS AND ADULTS

Chapter 10

ANSWERS TO QUESTIONS KIDS AND PARENTS MIGHT ASK

What does the word dyslexia mean?

The word dyslexia is the combination of two Greek word parts. **Dys** means difficulty and **lexia** means words. So, **dyslexia** means **difficulty with words**. However, it refers to very specific kinds of difficulty with words, like the kinds in this book. People with dyslexia have a lot of trouble reading and spelling words appropriate for their age even though they're smart, have had good teachers teaching them how to read and spell, and have tried really hard to learn.

How does dyslexia happen?

Scientists are still trying to answer this question. A human brain has about one hundred billion neurons in it — that's

100,000,000,000. Each of those neurons was made in just one part of the brain and had to travel to get to where it's supposed to be. Sometimes a few neurons get lost during the trip and end up in the wrong part of the brain. This happens before a person is born and is one reason why some people might have dyslexia. There can be more than one cause for reading and spelling problems. Maybe by the time you're grown up, we'll have better answers.

If I have dyslexia, does it mean my brain is broken or that I have brain damage?

No, your brain is definitely not broken and you do not have brain damage. Your brain is fine. It's just a little different from the brain of someone who is a good reader and speller. Everyone's brain is different. For example, I can read okay, but I can't sing, dance, or draw. I'm also not very good at sports, building things, or taking things apart and putting them back together. But, you're probably good at some of these things. So, your brain is different from mine, and your brain is fine. Your brain is normal, and so are you.

If I have dyslexia will it go away?

Scientists are trying to understand dyslexia better and are trying to find better ways to help people with dyslexia become good readers and spellers. So, the answer to this question may change as we find out more about dyslexia and how to help people with it. We know that you'll get better at reading and spelling if you have good teachers and if you keep trying really hard to learn and use what they're teaching you. We also know that you have to practice by reading as much as you can even though it might not be something you like to do. But, as far as we know right now, dyslexia doesn't go away. It's a part of who you are. However, some research shows that with the right help, the brains of some people with dyslexia actually change and begin to work more like the brains of average readers and spellers. So, maybe one day in the future scientists will find a way to make dyslexia go away.

Can dyslexia be fixed with eyeglasses or a hearing aid?

No, glasses and hearing aids won't get rid of dyslexia. Of course, you should have your vision and hearing checked to make sure they're okay. That's very important. You need to be able to see and hear. But people with dyslexia don't have trouble with words because of the way their eyes and ears work.

How does someone find out if they have dyslexia?

To find out if you have dyslexia you have to be tested by someone who knows a lot about it. This person is often a psy-chologist (sye-KOL-u-jist). Psychologists are usually called doctor, but they don't give kids shots like a medical doctor does. Instead, they talk with kids and give them tests. The tests help find out about things the kids do well and things that give them a hard time. Finding out why someone is having a hard time with reading and spelling is important, and no one wants to make a mistake, so these tests can take a long time. Many of the tests are just like things you do at school and none of them hurt, but your brain might get tired from all the hard work you'll need to do. Sometimes the tests happen at school, and sometimes kids need to go to the psychologist's office.

Are there other kinds of reading problems?

Yes, there are other kinds of reading problems other than the ones in this book. For example, some kids have a lot of trouble when they first learn to read and write, but they catch on as they get older and their reading problems go away. These kids don't have dyslexia. Some kids can have trouble with reading because of poor health, bad teaching, a lack of interest or motivation, vision or hearing problems, emotional or behavioral problems, growing up in homes where reading is not important or practiced, trying to learn a second language, or learning differences that are not dyslexia (such as attention deficit hyperactivity disorder, ADHD). Also, there might be other kinds of dyslexia besides the ones in this book. Scientists are still studying it and trying to understand it better.

I can remember the words to songs okay and I can remember what pictures look like, so, why can't I remember words and letters?

Brains are different from other parts of our bodies. Every part of an arm is made to move and lift things. Every part of a heart is made to pump blood. Every part of an eye is made to help you see. But brains are complicated. Each part of your brain has a special job to do. There is a part of your brain whose job is just to remember people's faces. There's another part of your brain whose job is just to remember what people look like when they walk, and a different part of your brain remembers what their voices sound like. Completely different parts of your brain are used to remember the name of the street you live on, the route to follow to get from your house to school, how to ride a bike so you can travel from your house to school, and what happened during your school recess yesterday. Still other parts of your brain are used to remember letters and words. In fact, different parts of your brain are responsible for remembering different types of words. Because our brains are so complicated, different people have strengths and weaknesses in different areas.

Can you tell me more about my brain?

People's brains start to be made before they're born. After people are born, their brains keep growing just like the rest of them, but they usually don't get new neurons. When you're born, your brain has all the neurons it needs to work. In fact, it has about twice as many as it needs! So, it has to get rid of the extras and figure out how to use the ones it keeps. Figuring out how to use all those brain cells takes a long time and is what learning is all about. Remember, you have to learn how to use about 100,000,000,000 neurons. No wonder you have to spend so much time in school! People's brains continue to mature until they're about 35 years old. But no matter how old you are, you never stop being able to learn.

You should also know that about 20 percent of the energy you get from food is used to run your brain. And, the more you think, the more you need to eat and drink to keep your brain running smoothly. So, be sure to bring snacks to school with you. Fresh and dried fruit make excellent snacks and provide a lot of energy for your brain. Water is also important, so you should bring that with you to school too.

If you want to know more about your brain and how it works, you can read books like these:

Farndon, J. (2000) *The Big Book of the Brain: All about the Body's Control Center.* Lincolnwood, IL: Peter Bedrick Books.

Parker, S. (2004) *The Brain and Nervous System.* Chicago, IL: Raintree.

Simon, S. (1999) *The Brain: Our Nervous System.* New York: HarperCollins.

How can I learn to tell a b from a d?

This can be really hard. One way to remember the difference is to make each of your hands into a "thumbs-up" sign. Keeping your thumbs up, put your knuckles together so your thumbs are facing each other. If you look carefully, your hands now look like a bed, with your left thumb being where your head goes and your right thumb being where your feet go. If you look carefully at your hands again, you'll see that your left hand is shaped like a **b** (the first letter in **bed**) and your right hand is shaped like a **d** (the last letter in **bed**).

There are also other things you can do. You can make the letters **b** and **d** out of different materials while talking about what they look like. You can draw them with crayon. You can make them with glue and then sprinkle the glue with glitter or sand. You can make them out of clay. You can even make them out of cookie dough, and then eat them! These are just a few examples, I'm sure you can come up with other fun ways to practice making these and other letters or numbers that confuse you.

Where can my family or I get more information?

If it has not happened already, you can talk with your teachers and the person who tested you. They might be able to tell you things about your strengths and weaknesses that you don't already know. (And you could probably tell them important things about you that they don't know!) Many kids find this useful because it helps them feel better about themselves. There are also many different books and articles to read if you or your parents want to know more. Some examples are listed below.

Clark, A.D. (2005) *Diseases and Disorders – Dyslexia.* Farmington Hills, MI: Thompson Gale (for upper middle school and older, including parents).

Frank, R. and Livingstone, K. (2002) *The Secret Life of the Dyslexic Child.* New York: Rodale (for adults).

Hultquist, A.M. (2006) *An Introduction to Dyslexia for Parents and Professionals.* London: Jessica Kingsley Publishers (for adults).

Kurnoff, S. (2000) *The Human Side of Dyslexia: 142 Interviews with Real People Telling Real Stories.* Monterey, CA: London Universal Publishing (for adults).

Levine, M. (1997) *The Mind That's Mine.* Chapel Hill, NC: All Kinds of Minds (for ages ten and older).

Levine, M. (1999) *The Language Parts Catalog*. Cambridge, MA: Educator's Publishing Service (for ages ten and older).

Levine, M. (2002) *A Mind at a Time*. New York: Simon & Schuster (for adults).

Minsky, M. (2003) *Greenwood Word Lists: One-Syllable Words*. Longmont, CO: Sopris West (for parents and teachers).

Moragne, W. (1997) *Dyslexia (The Millbrook Medical Library)*. Brookfield, CT: Millbrook Press (for upper middle school and older, including parents).

Raskind, M.H., Margalit, M. and Higgins, E.L. (2006) "'My LD": Children's voices on the internet.' *Learning Disabilities Quarterly, 29*, 4, 253–268 (for adults).

Shaywitz, S. (2003) *Overcoming Dyslexia: A New and Complete Science-based Program for Reading Problems at any Level*. New York: Vintage (for adults).

Silverstein, A., Silverstein, V. and Nunn, L. (2001) *Dyslexia (My Health)*. New York: Franklin Watts (for ages eight to ten).

Stern, J. and Ben-Ami, U. (1996) *Many Ways to Learn: Young People's Guide to Learning Disabilities*. Washington DC: Magination Press (for ages nine to thirteen or older).

Wilken, P.A. (1996) *How to Read with Your Children: Parent/Caregiver Guide*. Longmont, CO: Sopris West (for parents).

Wiltshire, P. (2003) *Dyslexia (Health Issues)*. New York: Raintree Steck-Vaugn (for ages ten and older).

Chapter 11

TWO ACTIVITIES FOR PARENTS AND CHILDREN TO DO TOGETHER TO WORK ON READING AND SPELLING

There are many different things that you can do to help your child become a better reader and speller. Some ideas are found in this book. There are also other books with more ideas, activities, and resources that you can use. However, exactly what skills to work on will depend on knowing just what your child's strengths and weaknesses are. Therefore, it is important to find out as much as you can from the person who tested your child or from your child's teachers before you begin any kind of work at home.

Reading to your child (Check It Out 10, p.53) and practicing reading speed (Check It Out 9, p.48) are important and could be done with almost any child with dyslexia. Other skills that many children need to practice are sounding out and spelling words. Therefore, I have provided an activity below that uses plastic letters and which you could do with your child. But remember to check with the professionals who know your child before you start so you can make sure your child is ready for the work I describe. Some children need to begin with the kind of activities listed in Check It Out 5 (p.31) before they are ready to read and spell. I have also provided a second technique for practicing spelling words.

Before you begin, there are three things you should know. First, there is more to teaching kids how to sound out and spell words than are covered by these activities. A qualified and trained educator should do such teaching. Second, the two activities I provide here should be supplemental to what happens at school. Therefore, you should coordinate what you are doing at home with what your child's teacher is doing. Finally, not every parent and child make a good team. Sometimes, parents and children just do not work well together. You should not force the issue. That is not pleasant for anyone and does not create a good learning environment.

Learning to sound out and spell words using plastic letters

Providing children with practice using their knowledge of letter–sound relationships is important. This helps them learn how to sound out and spell words they do not know. You could work with your child by using plastic letters. Some of them are magnetic and some are not. You can use either kind. Although most of the work you do will be with lower case letters, you might want to buy a set that has both upper and lower case letters in case you end up practicing proper names. You will also need to be sure that the set you buy contains more than one of each lower case letter.

Plastic letters are great to use because they are very visual and hands-on. In addition, you and your child get to move them around to make new words without having to write and erase. They can also help you show your child how she or he can use words and spelling patterns that she or he already knows to figure out new words. Spelling patterns are letter combinations that occur together in different words. One example of a spelling pattern is the **at** pattern that is used in words such as **hat**, **cat**, and **bat** as well as longer words such as **battle**, **doormat**, and **catalyst**.

To start, you could make a simple two- or three-letter word that your child can read. For example, you could use the plastic letters to make the word **man**. Have your child read the word to you. Then, you can change the first letter and have the child read the new word. So, you could take the **m** off of man and replace it with a **p** to make the word **pan**. If your child cannot read **pan**, tell her or him that this new word rhymes with **man** and ask what sound **p** makes.

You need to be careful when giving your child letter sounds. Many people do it incorrectly. For example, the letter **p** makes the sound /p/ and not "puh", the letter **m** makes the sound /mmmmm/ and not "muh", and the letter **f** makes the sound /fffff/ and not "fuh." You need to be very careful not to add the "uh" to the end of the letter. You might want to review letter sounds with a qualified reading specialist before you start to be sure you are doing it correctly.

Hopefully, your child will tell you that **p** makes the /p/ sound. If your child does not know the sound for **p**, tell her or him what the sound is. Next, ask your child for the word that rhymes with **man** and starts with the /p/ sound. If your child still cannot read the word, tell her or him what it is and have the child repeat it while looking at it. Then point out that the words **man** and **pan** rhyme because they both end with the /an/ sound. The only difference is in the first letter. Tell the child that if she or he can read **man**, it is possible to read **pan** by just changing the first sound. You could then put the **m** back, read the word **man** with the child, change the **m** to **p** again, and read **pan** together. (If your child cannot do this beginning activity, she or he might not know about rhyming or might not know letter sounds. Therefore, you might need to talk with her or his teacher to find out what skills you should work on first before continuing with this activity.)

Next, you could replace the **p** in **pan** with an **f** to make the word **fan**. Have your child try to read this word. If she or he cannot, tell her or him that it rhymes with **man** and **pan** and ask what sound **f** makes. Hopefully, your child will tell you that **f** makes the /f/ sound. If your child does not know the sound for **f**, tell her or him what the sound is. Next, ask your child for a word that rhymes with **man** and **pan**, and that starts with the /f/ sound. If your child still cannot read the word, tell her or him what it is and have the child repeat it while looking at it. Then talk some more about rhyming. Use the plastic letters to make the words **man**, **pan** and **fan** right under each other. Point out how all the words share the same two letters at the end. Talk about the sounds those letters make when they come together (/an/) and how this is what makes the words rhyme. Ask the child to tell you some other words that rhyme with **man**, **pan**, and **fan**. They do not have to be real words, as long as they rhyme. Then you could use the plastic letters to make those words. If your child cannot think of any rhyming words, you should offer some examples and spell them using the letters. Have your child practice reading the different words. Also practice making the different words by changing just the first letter.

It is good to practice creating, reading, and spelling made-up words. For example, if you practice with three-letter, low frequency and made-up words such as **mar** and **ket**, your child will be better prepared to spell a word like **market**.

After your child is able to read new words when you change just the first letter (and it is okay if the words you make are not always real words), you could work on changing the last letter. So, you could again spell **man** with the letters, but now change the **n** to a **d**. Have your child read the new word. Try to help her or him sound it out. If the child cannot, you should say the word broken into two parts while pointing to the letters. So, point to the **m** and say /m/. Then point to the **ad** and say /ad/ while running your finger under the letters. Ask your child to blend the sounds together. If she or he cannot, try it once more. If the child still cannot do it, say the word and have her or him repeat it. Then talk about what you changed and what sounds the letters make. (If your child cannot succeed with this, you should talk with her or his teachers to find out what skills you should work on first before continuing with this activity.)

You can practice changing the last letter in words just like you practiced changing the first letter. You can even practice changing the middle letter. For example, **man** could become **men**.

After your child gets good at these skills, you can add more sounds, such as changing the **m** in **man** to **sp** to make **span**. You can also change both the beginning and endings of words. For example, you could change the **m** in **man** to **st** and also add a **d** to the end to make the word **stand**.

There are many different spelling patterns you can use with your child. I have put lists of some of them later in this book (pp.85–88). There are also lists of changes you could make to the beginning and ending of words. These changes involve using letter combinations such as consonant blends, consonant digraphs, and other common letter groupings.

The words you work with could also have long vowels. When a vowel says its name, teachers often call it a **long vowel** or a **long vowel sound**. Remember the rule from Check It Out 7 (p.40) that when two vowels are next to each other, the first one says its name and the second one is silent? You could use the letters to make a word like **man** and then have your child figure out what the new word is after you change it to **main**. Another rule you could practice is the silent **e** rule. According to this rule, when there is a silent **e** at the end of a word, the vowel says its name. So, you could make the word **man** and then add an **e** to the end to make the word **mane**. (Be careful. As with any rule, this one is not perfect. For example, the words **love**, **prove**, **have**, and **glove** all end in a silent **e** but do not have long vowel sounds.)

You could also have your child change the letters to create new words that she or he would then read. You should definitely give your child words to spell using the letters. In this instance, you would say a word and the child would use the letters to make the whole word. You could also have your child make new words by changing just one letter. For example, have your child spell **man** with the letters. You could then say something like, "Okay, good job. Now change just one letter to make it say **pan**."

You do not have to stick with just one-syllable words. After your child knows how to read and spell one-syllable words, you can use the same spelling patterns to practice reading and spelling two-syllable words, such as **market**, **center**, **helmet**, **velvet**, **comfort**, **chapter**, **railroad**, **dislike**, **sailboat**, and so on. The more spelling patterns you practice, the more complex the words will be that you will be able to work on. For words of two or more syllables, you might want to start by having your child say and spell them one syllable at a time and then put the syllables together.

In addition to using the plastic letters, you can also use the words your child has learned in various games. For example, you could write them on index cards and use them in games such as Go Fish, War, and Concentration or Memory. You could also write sentences on larger index cards using the words, and then use those sentences with the board from a game such as Candy Land or Chutes and Ladders. The number of words each player reads correctly in their sentence would determine the number of spaces moved on the board.

How to practice spelling words using the simultaneous oral spelling method

Simultaneous oral spelling (or SOS) is one kind of multisensory technique that can be used to learn and practice spelling words. Since the focus here is on the names of letters and not their sounds, this is a good activity to use with irregular words. Irregular words are words that do not completely follow letter–sound or spelling rules. The words **come** and **said** are irregular because the rules say that they should have long vowel sounds, but they do not. The steps involved in SOS for words of one or two syllables are as follows:

1. Have your child read the word.

2. Have your child copy the word while saying the name of each letter
    as she or he writes it.

3. Have your child read the word again and check the spelling.

4. Have your child write the word from memory as she or he names
    each letter again.

5. Have your child read the word and check to be sure it is spelled
    correctly.

6. Repeat steps one through five twice more before moving on to the
    next word.

If your child can spell well enough to be working on words with three or more
syllables, the SOS procedure could be modified a little. For these longer words
proceed as follows:

1. Have your child read the word.

2. Have your child copy the word while saying each syllable as she or
    he writes it.

3. Have your child read the word again and check the spelling.

4. Have your child write the word from memory as she or he says each
    syllable again.

5. Have your child read the word and check to be sure it is spelled
    correctly.

6. Repeat steps one through five twice more before moving on to the
    next word.

After you are done, you might want to have your child write a sentence for
each of the words she or he practiced. This will provide her or him with experience using the words in a real-life activity. That kind of experience is important to help your child generalize the spellings she or he just learned to a new
situation. It is common for children to learn a skill in one setting, but be unable
to use that skill in a slightly different situation. That is why this kind of
writing practice is important. It is also why, if you study the words more than

once, you should do them in a different order every time. Some children learn how to spell words in a certain order but then cannot spell them if the words are dictated in a different order from the way they learned them. Finally, it is very important that your child be able to read the words that she or he is being asked to learn how to spell, and that she or he knows what they mean. For example, if your child is reading at a Grade 2 level but being asked to learn how to spell Grade 4 words, she or he may not remember them or use them.

Some spelling patterns and other letter combinations to practice with the plastic letters

For each spelling pattern or letter combination I have provided one word that uses those letters as an example. You should check with your child's teacher to find out what patterns and combinations are being worked on at school. Then you can reinforce what the teacher is doing by working on those same skills at home. I have listed only some spelling patterns and letter combinations, and they are in no particular order. Other books, or your child's teacher, could provide more comprehensive lists. One possible resource is the book *Greenwood Word Lists: One-Syllable Words* by Michael Minsky (see p.78).

Spelling patterns: short vowels

ab (cab)	ad (bad)	ag (bag)	al (pal)	am (jam)
an (man)	ap (nap)	as (has)	at (cat)	ax (wax)
ack (back)	act (fact)	aff (staff)	aft (raft)	alm (calm)
amp (camp)	and (band)	ang (bang)	ank (bank)	ant (pant)
ash (rash)	ask (mask)	asp (gasp)	ass (pass)	ast (fast)
ath (bath)	azz (jazz)	adge (badge)	atch (match)	
ed (bed)	eg (beg)	el (gel)	em (hem)	en (hen)
ep (pep)	es (yes)	et (met)	ex (vex)	ez (fez)
eck (deck)	eft (theft)	elf (shelf)	ell (cell)	elt (melt)
end (bend)	ent (rent)	ept (wept)	esh (fresh)	esk (desk)
ess (chess)	est (nest)	edge (hedge)	etch (stretch)	

ib (fib)	id (hid)	ig (big)	im (him)	in (bin)
ip (hip)	is (his)	it (sit)	ix (fix)	iz (quiz)
ick (kick)	iff (cliff)	ift (gift)	ilk (milk)	ill (fill)
ilt (tilt)	imp (limp)	ing (spring)	ink (mink)	int (mint)
ish (dish)	isk (disk)	isp (lisp)	iss (kiss)	ist (fist)
izz (fizz)	idge (ridge)	itch (hitch)		
ob (mob)	od (rod)	og (dog)	om (mom)	on (on)
op (hop)	ot (hot)	ox (box)	ock (clock)	off (scoff)
oft (soft)	oll (doll)	omp (romp)	ond (pond)	ong (song)
onk (honk)	osh (posh)	oss (boss)	ost (cost)	oth (broth)
odge (dodge)	otch (botch)			
ub (cub)	ud (mud)	ug (bug)	um (hum)	un (bun)
up (pup)	us (bus)	ut (but)	ux (tux)	uck (duck)
uff (cuff)	ull (skull)	ump (bump)	ung (sung)	unk (sunk)
unt (hunt)	ush (hush)	usk (dusk)	uss (fuss)	ust (bust)
uzz (buzz)	udge (budge)	utch (hutch)		

Spelling patterns: one vowel irregular patterns

The vowel should be short, but is not

all (ball)	ild (child)	ind (find)	old (bold)	oll (roll)
olt (bolt)	ost (most)	ull (bull)		

Spelling patterns: long vowels

ai (paid)	ay (day)	ea (beat)	ee (feet)	ie (pie)
oa (boat)	oe (doe)	ow (grow)	igh (high)	ight (right)
a-e (came)	e-e (theme)	i-e (like)	o-e (home)	u-e (cube)

Spelling patterns: vowel pair irregular patterns

The first vowel should be long, but is not

ea (head, bear, learn, heart)   ei (vein)   ie (field)   oa (oar)

Spelling patterns: vowel diphthongs and digraphs

au (caught)	ew (dew)	ew (few)	ew (sew)	oi (oil)
oo (book)	oo (door)	oo (food)	ou (mouse)	ou (soup)
ow (how)	ow (low)	oy (boy)	ue (blue)	ui (ruin)

Spelling patterns: r-controlled vowels

ar (car)   er (fern)   ir (bird)   or (horn)   ur (fur)

Spelling patterns: a few other vowel spelling patterns

aw (law)	awn (dawn)	e (he)	ey (grey)	ey (key)
o (no)	y (shy)			

Spelling patterns: beginning consonant blends

bl (black)	br (broom)	cl (clock)	cr (crew)	dr (drop)
fl (flow)	fr (frog)	gl (glow)	gr (grape)	kl (klutz)
kr (krill)	pl (plum)	pr (prune)	sc (scab)	scr (scrape)
sk (skate)	sl (slate)	sm (smell)	sn (snow)	sp (spurt)
spl (splat)	spr (spring)	st (stem)	str (string)	sw (swept)
tr (truck)	tw (twirl)			

Spelling patterns: beginning consonant digraphs and silent letter combinations

ch (chew)	kn (knock)	ph (photo)	sh (shack)	shr (shrub)
th (then)	th (thin)	thr (throw)	wh (while)	wr (wrote)

Spelling patterns: ending consonant blends and digraphs

ch (branch)	ck (back)	ct (fact)	ft (left)	lb (bulb)
lch (belch)	ld (held)	lf (gulf)	lk (milk)	lm (film)
lp (help)	lt (belt)	mp (stamp)	nch (punch)	nd (find)
nk (bank)	nt (went)	pt (kept)	rb (herb)	rch (perch)
rd (bird)	rf (scarf)	rk (cork)	rl (snarl)	rm (form)
rn (born)	rp (harp)	rsh (marsh)	rst (burst)	rt (start)
rth (birth)	sh (bush)	sk (ask)	sp (clasp)	st (dust)
tch (batch)				

Appendix

PROFESSIONAL ORGANIZATIONS

The presence of an organization on this list is not intended as either an endorsement or recommendation. While I made every effort to provide accurate contact information, I assume no responsibility for changes that occured during or after publication.

USA

Council for Exceptional Children
1110 North Glebe Road, Suite 300
Arlington, VA 22201–5704
Tel: 703 620 3660
TTY: 866 915 5000
Fax: 703 264 9494
Email: service@cec.sped.org
Website: www.cec.sped.org

Council for Learning Disabilities
11184 Antioch Road, Box 405
Overland Park, KS 66210
Tel: 913 491 1011
Fax: 913 491 1012
Email: CLDInfo@ie-events.com
Website: www.cldinternational.org

International Dyslexia Association
40 York Road, 4th floor
Baltimore, MD 21204
Tel: 410 296 0232
Fax: 410 321 5069
Voice message requests for information:
1-800-ABCD123
Website: www.interdys.org

Learning Disabilities Association of America
4156 Library Road
Pittsburgh, PA 15234
Tel: 412 341 1515
Fax: 412 344 0224
Email: info@ldaamerica.org
Website: www.ldanatl.org

Recording for the Blind & Dyslexic (RFB&D) (for textbooks on tape or CD)
20 Roszel Road
Princeton, NJ 08540
Tel: 866 732 3585
Website: www.rfbd.org

Australia

Dyslexia-SPELD Foundation WA (Inc)
PO Box 409
South Perth, WA 6951
Tel: 08 9217 2500
Fax: 08 9367 1145
Email: support@dyslexia-speld.com
Website: www.dyslexia-speld.com

SPELD NSW Inc
PO Box 332
West Belrose, NSW 2085
Tel: 02 9451 9477
Fax: 02 9451 9466
Email: enquiries@speldnsw.org.au
Website: www.speldnsw.org.au

SPELD Queensland Inc
PO Box 1238
Coorparoo, QLD 4151
Tel: 07 3394 2566 (1800 671 114 outside metro area)
Fax: 07 3394 2599
Email: speld@speld.org.au
Website: www.speld.org.au

SPELD South Australia
SPELD (SA) Inc
PO Box 83
Glenside, SA 5065
Tel: 08 8431 1655
Fax: 08 8364 5751
Email: info@speld-sa.org.au
Website: www.speld-sa.org.au

SPELD Tasmania Inc
PO Box 154
North Hobart, Tasmania 7002
Tel: 03 6275 0304

SPELD Victoria Inc
494 Brunswick Street
North Fitzroy
Melbourne, VIC 3068
Tel: 03 9489 4344
Fax: 03 9486 2437
Email: speldvicadmin@speldvic.org.au
Website: www.speldvic.org.au

Canada

Canadian Council for Exceptional Children
Website: canada.cec.sped.org

Canadian Dyslexia Association
207 Bayswater Avenue
Ottawa, Ontario K1Y 2G5
Tel: 613 722 2699
Fax: 613 722 4799
Email: info@dyslexiaassociation.ca
Website: www.dyslexiaassociation.ca

International Dyslexia Association
40 York Road, 4th Floor
Baltimore, MD 21204
Tel: 410 296 0232
Fax: 410 321 5069
Voice message requests for information:
1-800-ABCD123
Website: www.interdys.org

Learning Disabilities Association of Canada
250 City Centre Avenue, Suite 616
Ottawa, Ontario K1R 6K7
Tel: 613 238 5721
Fax: 613 235 5391
Email: information@ldac-taac.ca
Website: www.ldac-taac.ca

Hong Kong

Dyslexia Association
8 Crown Terrace
Pokfulam, Hong Kong
Email: info@dyslexia.org.hk
Website: www.dyslexia.org.hk

Ireland

Dyslexia Association of Ireland
1 Suffolk Street
Dublin 2
Tel: 01 6790276
Fax: 01 6790273
Email: info@dyslexia.ie
Website: www.dyslexia.ie

New Zealand

Learning and Behaviour Charitable Trust
PO Box 40–161
Upper Hutt
Website: www.lbctnz.co.nz

Learning Difficulties Coalition of New Zealand
PO Box 6748
Wellington
Tel: 04 382 8944
Fax: 04 382 8943
Email: ldc@paradise.net.nz
Website: www.ldc.co.nz

SPELD NZ
Website: www.speld.org.nz

United Kingdom

Bangor Dyslexia Unit
The Dyslexia Unit
University of Wales
Bangor, Gwynedd LL57 2DG
Tel: 01248 382 203
Fax: 01248 383 614
Email: dyslex-admin@bangor.ac.uk
Website: www.dyslexia.bangor.ac.uk

British Dyslexia Association
98 London Road
Reading, Berkshire RG1 5AU
Tel: 0118 966 2677
Fax: 0118 935 1927
Helpline: 0118 966 8271
Email: helpline@bdadyslexia.org.uk
Website: www.bdadyslexia.org.uk

British Dyslexia Association
Northern Ireland
Helpline: 02890 679 211
Website:
www.bdadyslexia.org.uk/nireland.html
Email: nihelpline@bdadyslexia.org.uk

Dyslexia Action
Website: www.dyslexiaaction.org.uk

Dyslexia Scotland
National helpline: 0844 800 84 84
Website: www.dyslexiascotland.org.uk

Prosiect Dyslecsia Cymru/Welsh
Dyslexia Project
Email: llechryd1@btconnect.com
Website: www.welshdyslexia.info

ABOUT
THE AUTHOR

Alan M. Hultquist, EdD is a licensed school psychologist with a doctorate in educational psychology. His ia also licenced as an elementary educator, special educator, and consulting teacher. He has worked with children professionally since 1979. He is a member of the American Psychological Association and the National Association of School Psychologists (United States). He is also the author of *An Introduction to Dyslexia for Parents and Professionals* published by Jessica Kingsley Publishers. He would like to thank the following people for taking the time to read and comment on earlier drafts of this book: Robin Stander, Kathy Johnson, Anne Stern, Lorna Murphy, Marie Manning, Paul Donahue, and of course, Brendan.

ABOUT
THE ILLUSTRATOR

Lydia T. Corrow has worked in the field of education for over 20 years. She holds degrees in Art Education and in Teaching English as a Second Language. Her pastimes include painting and weaving.

38704520R00055

Made in the USA
San Bernardino, CA
11 September 2016